Pray Now
2007

Daily Devotions for the Year 2007

Published on behalf of the

OFFICE FOR WORSHIP AND DOCTRINE,
MISSION AND DISCIPLESHIP COUNCIL,
THE CHURCH OF SCOTLAND

SAINT ANDREW PRESS
Edinburgh

First published in 2006 by
SAINT ANDREW PRESS
121 George Street, Edinburgh EH2 4YN

Copyright © Office for Worship and Doctrine, Mission and Discipleship Council, the Church of Scotland, 2006

10-digit ISBN 0 86153 375 5
13-digit ISBN 978 0 86153 375 6

British Library Cataloguing in Publication Data
A catalogue record for this book is available from the British Library

Typeset by Waverley Typesetters, Fakenham
Printed and bound in Germany by Bercker GmbH

Contents

Preface

We are all affected by the horizons of space. Near or far, whether seen with the eyes or shaped in the imagination, the horizons of physical geography are a part of how we understand ourselves and, moreover, where we encounter God. The Biblical witness, not surprisingly, makes reference again and again to location. Thus there is affirmation of human corporeality and of meeting-points with the Lord who is confined neither to time nor to space.

Pray Now 2007 explores how we might pray through this consciousness of space. As it is in many different places that the encounter with God has been nourished in times past, so in today's experience the divine invitation and inspiration will not be limited to church buildings, treasured though these may be. A common metaphor for Christian discipleship is the 'journey of faith'. The reflections and readings in the pages that follow encourage us to do more than sit still.

REV. DR PETER DONALD
Convener
Task Group on Worship and Doctrine
Mission and Discipleship Council

Using this Book and CD

31 days and eight sections

If you have used *Pray Now* before, you will notice again this year that the 31-day monthly pattern is there for those who like to go through the book from start to finish each month. However, the Pray Now Group are pleased to introduce a CD complement this year which not only provides a facility for those with visual impairment but also enables busy people to listen and reflect in the car, in the kitchen or wherever. The CD and book can be used together. You will notice that the 31 days – based on the theme 'landscapes' – have eight sections, and that each of these sections introduces a landscape that will be looked at for a few days in the monthly pattern. Those wishing to dip in and out of the book may wish to choose the landscape section they would like to reflect on, on any given day. The CD has eight tracks, one for each landscape section, including an introduction to each one to set the scene. We hope that readers and listeners will develop their prayer life in choosing the way that works best for them, be it in the 31-day pattern, in an eight-section pattern or in a mixture of reading and listening to different sections at different times.

Prayer for the Church

Each day, there is prayer for some aspect of the work of the Church universal. The example given in *italics* refers to that area of work as it is carried forward in the Church of Scotland, but it is expected that those from other branches of the Church will substitute their own material. Again, at the end of the book there is a list of Church of Scotland Mission Partners, each with the day on which they are to be prayed for. Members of other branches of the Church may wish to substitute similar persons or topics for prayer at that point.

The material should not be used slavishly but in the way that is most helpful. You may, for example, wish to substitute other prayers or readings, including the Lord's Prayer.

A daily lectionary

Included as an appendix is a separate list of daily Bible readings, based on the Scripture passages used in Church on Sunday by congregations that follow the lectionary in *Common*

Order (the internationally used Revised Common Lectionary). This daily version is taken from a Uniting Church in Australia publication, *With Love to the World*, which also includes notes on the readings. Information about obtaining this publication is included with the list of readings.

Bulk buying

A price reduction may be applied when congregations or presbyteries purchase multiple copies of Pr*ay Now*. Further information may be had from the Office for Worship and Doctrine, wordoc@cofscotland.org.uk, 0131-225 5722 ext. 359.

Days of the Month

Introduction to Wilderness

How can the experience of wilderness bring you life?

We may not think we have much experience of the wilderness, yet the moors of Scotland and Yorkshire and elsewhere – and mountainous areas – are just that.

This section gives you the chance to explore how this landscape describes aspects of the feelings and experiences of daily life, in particular to have the courage to face the apparent bleakness and to learn to recognise your reactions, your habitual patterns and deepen into familiarity thus learning to face this territory within yourself without fear and with growing confidence.

Very many testify that it is our ability to stay calm and confident in God during our wilderness times that gives an unshakeable foundation to prayer life.

WILDERNESS – SAND

Therefore from one person, and this one as good as dead, descendants were born 'as many as the stars of heaven and as the innumerable grains of sand by the seashore'

~ Hebrews 11:12 ~

Wilderness – a place of wonder, of expansion, of terror, of desolation;
Wilderness – a state that allows great potential to be born within us,
   yet often through utterly rigorous testing
That we truly question whether we will get through it;
Wilderness – a condition that calls out deep prayer from within us.

Wilderness – a place of un-ending-ness;
No clear end in sight;
Goals missing or never materialising;
Monotony of every day;
Slow, plodding, getting nowhere.
How many of our days are like this?

Sand, sand and more sand;
Barrenness, no purpose, no meaning.
And God said 'I will indeed bless you, and I will make your offspring as numerous as
   the stars of heaven and as the sand that is on the seashore.'
God speaks poetry and inspiration
   into the very fabric of the wilderness
God places a treasure, which invites a change of perspective that transforms unending
   desert into infinite potential – from lack and distress to hope and promise,
Even when I cannot see the promise fulfilled – yet.

Help me see the treasure in the 'sand' of my life;
Heal me, free me, turn me around to see the wonder in the tired, weary, monotonous
   aspects of my life now;
Expand my limited way of looking, my restricted feeling of myself,
And do this for others, too, who I now name and ask that they know your
   blessing. AMEN.

Readings

Genesis 22:15–23:1 *The Promise and first signs of fulfilment*
1 Kings 4:29–34 *Wisdom, heritage of the promise*
Hosea 1:7–11 *The Promise continues*
Hebrews 11:1–12 *New Testament recognition of the Promise*

Prayer Activity

As if in one hand, 'hold' the aspects of your life that feel like a wilderness in a negative way. In the other hand, 'hold' abundant aspects of your life. Let each aspect speak their truth: allow dialogue, both with each other and with Jesus.

Allow words of prayer to arise: of longing, of intention and of hope.

Prayer for the Church

Its mission partners working with churches overseas and sharing their concerns (see page oo) and those who work in this country to support church and people in other countries and to remove crippling debt

especially the HIV/AIDS Project, Jubilee Scotland and aid agencies.

Blessing

I trust in your purpose in my life
I trust in your promises in my life
I trust I will find my way
I trust.

WILDERNESS – FLOWERING

He brought us into this place and gave us this land, a land flowing with milk and honey;

~ Deuteronomy 26:9 ~

There is a hint of promise, O God,
in every wilderness;
a drop of water in every desert,
a river that flows between all rock,
a loving word in the hollowest silence,
a field of flowers where once the dust blew,
resurrection among the tombstones,

and it comes to those who wait:
a lifetime for some,
fed-up with wilderness,
as the ancient Israelites were.
Yet the word came,
the promise unfolded,
and a banquet of milk and honey was shared.

Creator, for those who endlessly wait for good news:
for healing, for peace, for love,
I pray;

and may my own prayer echo for them,
the promise they can no longer hear.
Let it voice in heaven the hope they long for,
carried on the scent of a meadowful of flowers.

Readings

Exodus 3:16–20 *God reveals the plan*
Isaiah 40:1–10 *Reshaping the wilderness*
Deuteronomy 27:1–8 *A place of rejoicing*
Isaiah 48:12–22 *Living like water from rock*

Prayer Activity

Reflect on some flowers you have in the house or in the garden or a picture in a magazine. Think about what the earth would be like without those flowers, how dull it may be, how unfulfilled it may look, what potential lay unused. Now pray for someone, someone who is having difficulty of some kind, a neighbour, a family member, a prisoner of conscience. May you see your prayer in the same way the earth sees her flowers.

Prayer for the Church

Those who speak for the Church and show the relevance of the Gospel for our life in society

especially the Church and Society Council and the Scottish Churches' Parliamentary Office.

Blessing

In every wilderness may you smell flowers,
In every desert may you see footprints,
In every rocky place may you hear rivers flow,
And may the God of all life daily bring you resurrection.

WILDERNESS – PROPHETS

God has spoken; who can but prophesy?
~ Amos 3:8 ~

Lord God, we thank you for the prophets of old
    Isaiah, Jeremiah, Ezekiel and the glorious rest:
men with a message; men who feared you but no other:
those who spoke of your plans and purposes –
        railing against idolatry and defection
        condemning the ills of society
        challenging the complacent
        arousing all to do justice, to love kindness
          and to walk humbly with you.

Lord God, we thank you for latter-day prophets.
    who also interpreted the times, discerned the future,
        a Martin Luther King … a George MacLeod
          who like the Old Testament prophets
    had a dream, a vision, that gave hope and comfort
        not least as they witnessed to Jesus:
          the Messiah, the Christ, promised of old.

Lord God, we thank you for John the Baptist,
    the wild wilderness preacher
the last of the old prophets; the first to proclaim Jesus:
    the Lamb of God who takes away the sin of the world.
We thank you for all who preach your living Word
    with all who often, in some dry desert place,
        witness to Jesus:
on whom was laid the iniquity of us all.

Lord God, thanking you, above all, for him:
    whose chastisement made us whole,
    with whose stripes we are healed:
        Jesus Christ the supreme prophet,
    who can lead us through every wilderness,
    speak to men and women in our day
        and raise up many who will prophesy
        and proclaim your Word in Christ.   AMEN.

Readings

Deuteronomy 8:1–10   *Wilderness mercies*
Isaiah 6:1–8   *Isaiah Temple vision and call*
Mark 1:1–8   *John the Baptist in the wilderness*

Prayer Activity

Recall Isaiah's temple vision and the question: 'Who will go for us?' Think of some need within the Church or without: can you say 'Here am I, send me'?

Prayer for the Church

Those who monitor developments in human knowledge and bring the insights of the Gospel to bear so that new discoveries might be used wisely

especially the Society, Religion and Technology Project and the Eco-congregation Project.

Blessing

Guide me, O thou great Redeemer,
Pilgrim through this barren land;
I am weak but thou art mighty;
Hold me with thy powerful hand.   AMEN.

(William Williams 1717–91)

WILDERNESS – WANDERING

Sarah saw the son of Hagar the Egyptian, whom she had borne to Abraham, playing with her son Isaac. So she said to Abraham, 'Cast out this slave woman with her son; for the son of this slave woman shall not inherit along with my son Isaac.'

~ Genesis 21:9, 10 ~

Pilgrim God:

Ishmael was the son
Of Abram's impatience,
The hapless child
Of his unwillingness
To wait in the howling wilderness
Of the not-yet fulfilled promise.

Ishmael and his mother were the victims,
The collateral damage
Of a botched attempt
To accelerate the pace
Of your unfolding purposes.

Help me to see, Lord,
That there are times
When to act is to be disobedient,
That there are times
When to run ahead
Is to fall hopelessly behind.

Today, I remember all those who must
Learn the way of patient obedience;
Who find themselves stranded
In the featureless desert,
In the twilight world, the 'not yet'
Of your covenant promise.   AMEN.

Readings

1 Kings 19:1–10   *Elijah in a physical and spiritual wilderness*
Matthew 4:1–11   *Jesus is tempted in the wilderness*
Galatians 1:13–17   *Paul's wilderness preparation*
Exodus 3:1–6   *Moses at the burning bush*
Luke 3:1–9   *A voice crying in the wilderness*
Isaiah 35:1–11   *The wilderness transformed*

Prayer Activity

In Biblical terms, the 'desert' is the place of prayer, the hidden place of *being* behind the busy place of *doing*. We can see this pattern clearly in Jesus' ministry. A Russian word, 'poustinia' (meaning 'desert') refers to the place of quiet, of withdrawal, of prayer. Set apart somewhere in your house or garden as a 'poustinia'. Place there some objects as a focus for prayer – an open Bible, a cross, or perhaps some photographs of people you pray for.

Prayer for the Church

Those who witness to the living Christ in the midst of his people, in Word and Sacrament, those who as deacons lead the Church in living out the Gospel, and those who recruit, train and support them

especially the Ministries Council.

Blessing

The Lord of the journey,
The humble pilgrim of the road,
Keep you upon the right paths
In all your coming and going
Until your travelling days are done
And you see him face to face.

Introduction to Sea

Sea is more than water. Whichever way you look at it, it is our greatest source of stories and fears and miracles. One night a saviour walked on it and called his closest disciple to follow him in a never-tried-before adventure. Another time, that same disciple hauled in a catch mightier than any catch ever caught; all 153 species of fish that the sea could ever give. And the net held them all. Still, as then, the sea holds awe for us in its hidden depths and its mighty power. It calls to us like some ancient mother that birthed creation, and maybe we are attracted to it, with reverance and fear, because it holds our story; of birth and escape, of life and of death, of power and adventure. It is not a beginning, nor is it an end. It is simply always being; great, mighty and mysterious, as only God can be. Yet, in its being, it shapes for us our life, our seasons, the miracle of our home in this universe. God is, like the sea, always around us, supporting us and defying us.

SEA – WATER OF LIFE

With joy you will draw water from the wells of salvation.

~ Isaiah 12:3 ~

God of the ocean depths and awesome space of the sea,
God of the overwhelming wave and ice-sculpted landscape,
God of the flood that can damage, wash away and drown,
God of the down-pour – life growing and aiding, life enhancing and blessing …
Today we give thanks for the power of water.

Help us today to see another kind of power in water –
Shown in Jesus – the water of life.
Help us to realise that power in life and death, in sickness and in health –
Rivers to cross, pools to swim in,
Gardens to sprinkle, ponds to fish
Cleansing showers and soothing baths,
Diluted solutions and medicines swallowed,
Cold wet cloths on fevered heads,
Fresh washed clothes and food prepared and cooked,
Drinks that quench thirst and celebrate news,
Tears welling up, fonts gathered round.

God, in it all, we find you and are refreshed.

Readings

Psalm 36:5–8   *God's goodness and graciousness*
Revelation 7:13–17   *A vision of eternity*
John 4:1–15   *The woman at the well*

Prayer Activity

Some churches have 'soaking services' where people are encouraged to soak in the Spirit of God, to feel God's presence wash over them and surround them and comfort them. Today, feel God's presence flow over you every time you use water.

Prayer for the Church

The Church as it takes shape in areas where there are special difficulties – social, economic or health-related

especially the Mission and Discipleship Council in its work in mission and evangelism, worship, doctrine, education and nurture.

Blessing

> Water, water of life
> Wash me – pour afresh on me.
> Fill me – bring me life anew.
> I quench my thirst in you.

SEA – WALKING ON WATER

He came towards them early in the morning walking on the sea.

~ Mark 6:48 ~

God, it seems your kingdom works the wrong way round.

We scratch out order and design in this world
and call it religion
yet find you in the uncharted.

Our holiness is found in routine
in well worked out creeds
and fine constructed buildings
and we call it faith
yet find you in the unpredictable.

We build sanctuaries that beautify symmetry
creating a space that restrains the unfamiliar
and call it your realm
yet you are found outside the boat.

May our fear of the unexplored
be tempered by your voice through the confusion.
May our longing for solid ground
be balanced by your call amid the waves.
May our need for a boat
be lessened by your presence on the water
and may our faith be not safe
but risky
that we dare to step into the unknown
and find you where adventures are made.

Readings

> Matthew 14:22–32   *Jesus walks on water*
> Philippians 1:19–26   *Courage to go on*
> Hebrews 3:1–6   *Fix your thoughts on Jesus*
> 1 John 3:19–24   *Courage before God*

Prayer Activity

Think of an adventure, a time you were away from the normal routine. It may have been in a place you were unfamiliar with or somewhere you know very well, but something different happened. Stay with that adventure and reflect on a moment when you felt God's presence. Linger there remembering it. Spend some time remembering and enjoying the memory. How does that help your day? Appreciate the memory.

Prayer for the Church

Those who ensure that the local church is well supported and staffed and who take initiatives in mission and outreach where people live, work and take leisure

especially the Priority Areas Fund, and chaplaincies in hospitals, education, industry, prisons and residential homes.

Blessing

When you step out the boat, may God be holding you.
When you walk into darkness, may you walk into God.
When you find yourself in the unknown, may you find God beside you.
and, hand in hand, may you walk into the adventure of life, together.

SEA – DROWNING

Then the Lord spoke to the fish, and it spewed Jonah out upon the dry land.
~ Jonah 2:10 ~

Lord,
Out of the dark place,
Out of the constricting place,
Out of the disturbing place,

Jonah was re-born,
Given back life,
Given back hope,
Given back purpose.

From the depths,
He returned to the surface.
From his fear
He was released for faith.

In Jonah, you show me

That

Even in my rebellion –
Even in my disobedience
Even in my fear

I can be re-born into life and hope.

Today I pray for the Church:
So often imprisoned in fear
And held fast in the grip
Of remembered failure …

Show us, Lord,
That even our fear and failure
Can become the womb
From which a new day is born.

Readings

Prayer Activity

Jonah was 'imprisoned' in the belly of the great fish. (Some biblical scholars have taken this to be a symbol of the deportation to Babylon which 'swallowed up' the Jews when Jerusalem was destroyed in 587 BC.) Make a collection of cuttings of prisoners of conscience. Place these in your prayer corner and use them as a focus for prayer.

Prayer for the Church

As it explores and renews its faith in the contemporary context and lifts the world and its people to God in praise and prayer

especially all engaged in leading and planning worship, and those who study and write about what Christians believe.

Blessing

Know that God is with you
in the dark place and in the bright place,
in the cave and on the mountain top,
in your tears and
in your laughter.

SEA – CATCHING

Out of the depths I cry to you, O Lord.

~ Psalm 130:1 ~

The sea
The most mysterious place on earth
New plants, new creatures still being discovered
Treasure in the deep

Yet I resist going into my depths
Fear keeps me from possible wonder, delight and resource

And you, God, understand this
And Scripture both reflects this, and challenges me
'Do not be afraid' said so frequently
As acknowledgement and a call to freedom.
May I, like Peter, be prepared to have a go at things
Find myself occasionally out of my depths
But remain with my commitment – willing to recognise and run to God

And also willing to reflect on such memories
Prepared to ponder hidden depths
Opening myself to consider such mysteries as the huge catch of fish

Whether the waves in my life are calm or wild today
May I ride them
And know that the tide always turns …

Readings

Luke 5:1–11 *A previous catch*
Isaiah 45:1–8 *Treasures of darkness*
1 Samuel 12:16–25 *God who teaches rather than condemning*
Psalm 38 *God come close to me when I fail*

Prayer Activity

Jesus later in the story re-affirms Peter's call, reassures him. At the shore, sea and waves have rhythm that is often soothing in the midst of inner turmoil. Try repeating to yourself a prayer that has rhythm and reminds each of us of our call.

Lord Jesus Christ, Here I am
Breathe in 'Lord Jesus Christ', breathe out 'Here I am'. Allow your breath to slow down naturally.

Prayer for the Church

As it explores and renews its faith in the contemporary context and lifts the world and its people to God in praise and prayer

especially the Scottish Storytelling Centre and the wider work of the Netherbow.

Blessing

Hear God's call
Of love for you
Of value for you
Of challenge to you
Catching you into this day.

Introduction to Mountain

Mountains are really important in the Bible. Indeed, you might say that 'the mountain' is one of the Bible's key symbols. The mountain is the place of unveiling, of revelation.

And yet, in the Bible no-one is allowed to stay with the mountain-top experience. The mountain, as well as a revealing place, is always a sending place. From all our mountain-top experiences we are summoned back to the tangled realities of life in the valleys.

MOUNTAIN – CLIMBING

I lift up my eyes to the hills. From whence does my help come?
My help comes from the Lord, who made heaven and earth.

~ Psalm 121:1, 2 ~

We recall the mountains and hills of the Old Testament:
Ararat – where the Ark came to rest.
Sinai – where the Commandments were given.
Zion – on which Jerusalem is built.
Hermon – whose dews water the Holy Land …
Such high and holy places prompt us – to pause and wonder and give praise!

We recall the mountains and hills of the New Testament:
The Mount – where Jesus spoke the Beatitudes.
The hills – where he withdrew to pray.
The little hill of Calvary – where he died for us
The mountain of Galilee – where, risen, he left his disciples …
Such high and holy places prompt us – to pause and wonder and give praise!

We recall the mountains and hills we have known:
Their rugged majesty, their steadfast beauty
The fulfilment felt as the top was reached
A different perspective gained, another world sensed …
Such high and holy places prompt us – to pause and wonder and give praise!

Today, we recall that mountain where Jesus was transfigured,
give us also a vision of majesty eternal.
As climbers attempt a mountain because it is there,
help us to attempt the mountain of faith
and know that You are there:
greater than any mountain, higher than any hill
with your glory in Christ
whose vision can transfigure us
and make us holy as he is holy.
So help us, God over all.   AMEN.

Readings

Exodus 34:29–35 *Moses' shining face*
2 Peter 1:16–19 *Eye-witnesses to Christ's majesty*
Matthew 17:1–8 *The Transfiguration*

Prayer Activity

Take 'time out'; get away from the everyday. Climb or imagine some hill-top. Quietly commune with God. Thrill in the encounter at such a place. Then, with fresh vision and new perspective, come down again to live again.

Prayer for the Church

Those who bring their creativity to bear on making known the Gospel, in print, film, news media, sound and website

especially Saint Andrew Press, Life & Work, the Publishing Committee, and those who maintain the Church's website.

Blessing

Make us thy mountaineers;
We would not linger on the lower slope,
Fill us afresh with hope, O God of Hope,
That undefeated we may climb the hill
As seeing Him who is invisible.   AMEN.

Amy Carmichael (1867–1951) from *Towards Jerusalem* (SPCK, 1967)

MOUNTAIN – VIEW

'This is the land of which I swore to Abraham, to Isaac, and to Jacob, "I will give it to your descendants"; I have let you see it with your eyes but you shall not cross over there.'

~ Deuteronomy 34:4 ~

God,
what are we to do when we see the horizon,
but know we'll never arrive at it;
when we are called to hold and care for a promise
only a future generation will see fulfilled;
when we are asked to pass on the story for someone not yet born
not knowing if they will ever come to hear it?

Grant encouragement to your daily workers.
Gift the faith to recognise you are always found in the journeying,
that the learning is done in the travelling,
that signs and wonders unfold in every turn,
and the vision of your realm is made real only on the pathway.

May we go always in promise,
with confidence that every journey in life
is heading somewhere beautiful,
overflowing with milk and honey,
that we will one day call home.

So hear this prayer for those who journey without knowing where,
for life travellers weary of the journey,
for those with no purpose in their step and no trust in arriving,
that they all may find at the last,
your promise that is theirs,
and the love that will welcome them
home.

Readings

Deuteronomy 8:1–10   *The Land is near*
Deuteronomy 34:1–8   *Moses sees the Promised Land*
Isaiah 35:1–10   *The road home*
Revelation 21:1–4   *The new heaven and earth*

Prayer Activity

If you can, find an old photograph of your parents or grandparents. Reflect on what they taught you, or a phrase they always used to use, or a journey you went on with them. Think of their world, and how different it was to your own. What things have grown in you because of their care for you? Give thanks for those things and pray for those things we are entrusted with, for children you know today, who will be adults soon.

Prayer for the Church

Those who bring care and encouragement to people in any kind of need and who work for a healthier society in which all may find fulfilment

especially the Social Care Council, CrossReach, and the staff of the various units it operates.

Blessing

What you carry today,
is the gift for tomorrow.
What you speak of today,
will shape tomorrow.
And what you love today,
will bless every tomorrow.

MOUNTAIN – PRESENCE

'Come, let us go up to the mountain of the Lord …that he may teach us his ways and we may walk in his paths.'

~ Micah 4:2 ~

Immortal, invisible, God only wise:
  so far beyond me, so near to me
  with your love in Jesus your Son -
as I thank you for the commandments of old:
  laws given for my good on Mount Sinai,
    I confess that down in life's valley,
    I have ignored or broken them;
  and that sometimes they have broken me –
  made me less than what I could be.

Living God, forgive me
  for not taking rest from work and not taking time out for worship.
Forgive me from turning aside to other gods:
  gods of human making:
    power & pounds; sex & success; money & machines.
Forgive me for venerating such false idols.
Forgive me for thinking and speaking against my neighbours,
  and for any envy of their good fortune;
  and for not thinking and doing enough for those near to me.
Maybe I do not kill or commit adultery or steal,
  but forgive me for murderous and lustful feelings
  as for thinking I might take something that is not mine
And, Lord God, forgive me for breaking
  the new commandment, given by your Son:
  to love others … even my enemies.

Merciful God, set Christ's Cross between my souls and my sins …
  as I am contrite, assure me by the Holy Spirit that I am
  pardoned, healed, restored, forgiven.
And by Christ's grace raise me to new heights
  of fresh obedience and good and glorious living. AMEN.

Readings

Exodus 19:16–25   *Moses meets God on Mount Sinai*
Exodus 20:1–17   *The Ten Commandments*
Mark 10:17–22   *Jesus and the rich young ruler*

Prayer Activity

As you might stand on a mountain and survey everything take time to survey your life and how you might better live it. With fresh vision of what could be, descend to the valley of everyday life and in God's strength attempt it!

Prayer for the Church

Those who help us to take our place in, and be enriched by, the experience and witness of the Church throughout the world

especially the World Mission Council, Scottish Churches' World Exchange, and St Colm's International House, Edinburgh.

Blessing

As the Ten Commandments were engraved in tablets of stone,
write your Word in my heart and my mind –
especially that Word of love that was and is in Christ
who died and rose for me and for all.
So bless me this day.   AMEN.

MOUNTAIN – BLESSING

The spirit of God has made me, and the breath of the Almighty gives me life.

~ Job 33:4 ~

Told on a mountain – traditionally a place of meeting with God
Told as a series blessing – blessings that turned normal expectations upside down
Told at the beginning of his ministry – in a form that held echoes of the book of
    Deuteronomy

Blessed are those who are poor in spirit
Who rely on God for their breath, for their inspiration

Blessed are those who mourn, for they shall be comforted
Who open up to their emotions in a safe way, facing their truth and the pain
Feeling their depths, waiting and watching

Blessed are the meek, for they shall inherit the earth
Who discover and digest the truth of our smallness in the grand scheme of things

Blessed are those who hunger and thirst for righteousness, they shall be filled
Who honour the longing inside for truth and justice for ourselves and others

Blessed are the merciful, for they shall obtain mercy
Who embrace God into their very depths, into the womb of their being
Enabling an expansion of love, born of darkness within us
A wellspring of the living God

Blessed are the pure in heart, for they shall see God
Who are prepared to work through pain that confronts us in our lives
Willing to go into the depths and chaotic unknowns and still hold faith in Divine love
Then something within us increases our intimacy, our seeing the one who made us.

Blessed are the peacemakers, for they will be called the children of God
Who make space, and take time to allow the experience of love, joy and hope
Helping people to know that we all belong, that we are all loved, all valuable
Called into relationship with the One who made us

Blessed are those who are persecuted because of righteousness, for theirs is the
    Kingdom of heaven.

Blessed are you when people revile and hate you, your reward is great in the Kingdom
of heaven
Who learn truly to not be affected by other people's expectations and demands
Able to tolerate the backlash of disrupting, settled patterns that no longer give life
And willing to let go even of our own image of ourselves
So that your Presence moulds us so much we are able to push through unnecessary
boundaries
Living heaven here on earth. AMEN.

Readings

Prayer Activity

It is very easy for us to focus on our problems and so close ourselves off from
God's loving presence. Remember a recent example with God or with a person.
Examine what it feels like to close off, paying particular attention to how your body
feels. How do you know you have closed yourself? Remember a recent example
of feeling an opening up to God or a person. Again, pay attention to the changes
in you body. How do you sense that you have opened? Do you experience this
feeling of opening as a blessing?

Prayer for the Church

Those who seek to renew the life and mission of the Church, develop strategies and
establish priorities

*especially the Council of Assembly, the Panel for Review and Reform, and the Church
without Walls initiative.*

Blessing

Holy Spirit, Holy Breath
Always blessing – every breath
Breath in me, Spirit life.

Introduction to Trees

Without trees we could not live. Deforestation is making us more and more aware that the balance of our planet is delicately held. We need trees to hold the soil, we need trees to keep the atmosphere in balance so we can breath. Our need for trees seems to have been understood and appreciated by our ancestors in lots of ways

In the Bible, trees are commended for offering shade, giving us food, providing building material and creating warmth. Trees usually outlive us and thus they are often used as a symbol of, or metaphor for, stability, reliability and continuity.

Trees are also used as a motif to describe life – Tree of Jesse, Tree of Life. They are present at the beginning of time in the garden of Eden, in the turning point of Jesus' life on which he was crucified and at the end of time bringing healing. They journey with us theologically – and sometimes we still cannot see the wood for the trees.

TREES – GROWING

They are like trees planted by streams of water, which yields their fruit in its season.

~ Psalm 1:3 ~

Lord, just as Solomon built the Temple from cedars
You invite me
to allow you to build your temple within me.
Just as Solomon ordered the best wood, the Cedars of Lebanon
May I grow
the best I can for you, straight and strong

Just as the cedars embodied your majesty
You invite me
to let your love be in every fibre of my very being.
Just as the cedars spoke to people of your glory
May I let
your light shine through me

Just as their wood created sacred space
You invite me
to be moulded to create more room for your Presence.
Just as their wood exuded a beautiful smell
May I bring
the fragrance of your love to others

Following Jesus, who helps us understand that our bodies
are temples
of the living God.   AMEN.

Readings

Psalm 92	*We are described by comparison with trees*
Ezekial 31:1–14	*The majesty of the cedar tree given as a warning*
2 Samuel 5:9–12	*David, blessed by God, his house built of cedar wood*
1 Kings 5:1–12	*Building the Temple and securing cedar wood*
Matthew 3:7–12	*John the Baptist compares our lives to trees*
John 2:17–22	*Jesus speaks of his body as a temple*

Prayer Activity

Become aware of your breathing and your heartbeat. Reflect on the miracle that so much happens in your body without your needing to be conscious of the detail. Reflect that God has placed the Holy Spirit within you that works without your needing to understand also, creating a temple for the Living God.

Prayer for the Church

As it meets in councils and assemblies to listen to God and one another

especially the Assembly Arrangements Committee, the Nomination Committee, the Moderator, the Moderator Designate, the Principal Clerk and the Depute Clerk.

Blessing

May I house God today
In a way that feeds me and brings me blessing
May I house God today
In a way that feeds others and opens doors that they receive blessing.

TREES – LOST

He was trying to see who Jesus was, but on account of the crowd he could not, because he was short in stature. So he ran ahead and climbed a sycamore tree.

~ Luke 19:3–4 ~

Feeling low in every sense, insecure in being and crushed by a crowd giving no
   recognition or care – God we can imagine so well how Zacchaeus felt that day.

Confronted with his own deceit and bad track record,
oppressed by the fear that this was how it was always going to be,
Zacchaeus sensed your presence as an opportunity to rise above.

So let us have that kind of moment today God.
Let us climb out of the depths to see who you are
And in our shame and worry may we find that half-way house,
That secure branch to grab hold of,
That safe place to sit,
until you lovingly call to us, to finally let you in.

And help us too God to be rooted in your strength for others:
To be people they lean on
Places they shelter
Life they connect to.
That they too will see Jesus – in us.   AMEN.

Readings

> Luke 19:1–10   *The full story*
> 1 Samuel 14:24–30   *Forest fear*
> 2 Samuel 18:1–8   *Forest battle*

Prayer Activity

Hold a piece of wood in your hand. Look at its grain, its colour, its shape. Now imagine that small piece as part of the large tree it came from – where did it grow? What did it look like? What happened around it? Offer a prayer now for the Christian community you are part of – and reflect on the tree as a symbol of the church.

Prayer for the Church

Those who guide and administer the details of the Church's life at national level

especially the Central Services Committee, and all who look after the welfare of pensioners and the retired.

Blessing

> The posibilities of forgiveness,
> The strength of life,
> The root of love
> Be shown in you this day
> For Christ's sake.

TREES – DAVID IN HIDING

When Saul returned from following the Philistines, he was told, 'David is in the wilderness of Engedi.' Then Saul took three thousand chosen men out of all Israel, and went to look for David and his men in the direction of the Rocks of the Wild Goats.

~ 1 Samuel 24:1–2 ~

Lord,
hiding in the hills,
amongst forest, in caves,
was David, your chosen one,
Your anointed King,
Called and set apart
For the doing of your will.

Yet, his first palace
Was the wilderness,
And his first throne
The hard ground.

To be chosen by you
Was to be hated by Saul;
To be appointed by you
Was to be hounded by your enemies.

In David I see foreshadowed another King
Who had nowhere to lay his head,
Who became the friend of the dispossessed
And the champion of the marginalised.

Today I remember all
Who live on the edge,
I remember those who are persecuted for their faith
Or for their passion for justice and peace,
And for whom loyalty to their vocation
Means tension and enmity with those around them.

Bible Readings

1 Samuel 18:6–9	*Saul's growing jealousy of David*
Matthew 2:1–4	*Herod and the birth of Christ*
Luke 4:16–19	*The manifesto of the Servant King*
Psalm 13	*A prayer in time of persecution*
Matthew 8:18–22	*Jesus and the call to discipleship*
1 Samuel 26:6–13	*David refuses to kill his enemy*

Prayer Activity

When we are stressed, our breathing often becomes shallow and fast. This prayer exercise can be helpful at such moments both in slowing and deepening our breathing and in making us aware of the presence of God.

Focus on your breathing, say within yourself in rhythm with your breathing: 'Be still/and know/that I/am God.' Repeat this over and over for at least five minutes. Allow your breathing to gradually deepen and slow down, but do not force it unnaturally. The beauty of this exercise is that it can be done anywhere: before an exam, at the bus-stop, before a difficult meeting, or in church before the service begins.

Prayer for the Church

Those who guide the Church in temporal matters and see that, in its dealings, justice prevails

especially the Law Department and the Safeguarding Unit.

Blessing

Calm me O Lord as you stilled the storm,
Still me O Lord, keep me from harm,
Let all the tumult within me cease,
Enfold me Lord in your peace.

David Adam, *Borderlands*, p. 3 (SPCK, 1991)

TREES – COMMUNION

You will go out with joy and be led forth in peace … and the trees of the field will clap their hands.

~ Isaiah 55:12 ~

I give thanks for the beauty of the trees around me.
As I listen to the feelings evoked in me by trees
I feel joy, exuberance and delight
And feel connected with trees clapping their hands,
All creation praising you
And uplifting me
When I listen.

When I brush under natural arches
I feel welcomed, affirmed and special.
When I walk in a cathedral of trees
I rejoice.

Feeling deep connection with these trees that have been here for several generations,
Spanning time and still living,
Speaking to me of beauty, life and growth even across centuries,
And of your faithfulness to us in a cycle of nature that continues
Year after year
Nourishment and beauty intermingled.

And connection with people from Biblical times who like me
Rejoiced with trees
And connection with people who built cathedrals
Embodying, reflecting trees.

Keep us vigilant, Lord, to listen to nature around us
Keep us aware of the delicate balance now imperilled
Keep us from further abuse of the interconnectedness that gives us life. AMEN.

Readings

Judges 9:6–15   *A wisdom story about trees*
1 Kings 6:29–36   *Trees in the fabric and design of the Temple*
Isaiah 55:9–13   *Joy, peace and praise in all creation*
Luke 21:29–38   *Jesus invites us to listen and learn from trees*

Prayer Activity

Look at a tree. Notice qualities which it embodies: strength, flexibility, colour, shape. Allow these qualities to be present within you, flowing between you and the tree; rejoice in this communion with God's creation and let words of prayer flow.

Prayer for the Church

Those engaged in new, creative ministries and those who faithfully and energetically serve the parishes of our Lord.

Blessing

Keep the root of my life well nourished
The trunk of my life stable and strong
The branches of my being – stretching upwards and outwards
Yearning for new heights and song.

Introduction to Valley

At times, plains in the Bible are places where battles have been fought. Valleys are sometimes associated with darkness, and even with death. However, it was down from the hills to the flatter places that Jesus called his disciples, where crowds followed him, where he healed and helped, where so much of his loving activity took place. Glens, straths, howes and lower-lying lands are, by and large, where people work and where they live. Christianity has less to do with places and more to do with people – people where they are. 'All life is meeting', said a philosopher. Full life is meeting and, in today's world, as we live and work, Jesus meets us where we are and how we are, to give us the life we have often lost.

VALLEY – FERTILITY

Every valley shall be lifted up …
~ Isaiah 40:4 ~

O God, often, often we want you to come down –-
    some glorious cataclysm:
    an end to human hunger and suffering;
    an end to tyranny and terrorism;
    people, acknowledging you, raised
        from valleys of despair
        to bright mountains of hope.
Yet, praise be, that kingdom has begun:
    in Christ your glory was and is revealed.

We thank You that in Him
    we are given the new creation for a new world;
    a promise for peace and plenty;
    an agenda for a new age.
Forgive us for our failure to attempt it.
    The farmer has to tend the seed,
        but we have not attended your will;
            the seeds of Christ's planting often lie dormant;
            the seed of his redeeming Word has not been well sown.

O God our Father who gives life to the seed,
    speed the plough – that there may be a harvest for all;
    speed the Church – that your Word may be widely sown;
    and speed us – that we may bear fruit in our living:
        so may the valleys rejoice
        and the Kingdom come.   AMEN.

Readings

Psalm 65:9–13   *God's bounty in the harvest*
Galatians 5:22–6   *The fruit of the Spirit*
Luke 8:4–15   *The parable of the sower*

Prayer Activity

Observe and marvel at the growth of seeds planted in good ground. Ask if you are sufficiently planted 'in Christ' and are open enough to the outpouring of the Spirit.

Prayer for the Church

The organisations of women and men who worship, study and take the lead in reaching out to others

especially the Church of Scotland Guild.

Blessing

Lord of the harvest, bless the seed and bless the sower;
exalt the plains and valleys in fertility –
    with all given their daily bread.
Prosper the proclamation of your Word –
    with many raised from the valleys to the heights.
And help us, abiding in Christ, to bear much fruit.   AMEN.

VALLEY – RIVER CROSSING

As soon as the priests stepped into the river, the water stopped flowing.

~ Joshua 3:15–16 ~

Living God,
if we never go down into the valley
and get our feet wet as we step into the river,
then we will never know what it is
to risk everything,
and trust everything to your promises.

If we never go down into the valley
and face the Jordan
getting our feet wet,
then we will never know what it is
to imperil our faith,
and discover, deeper still, the certainty of love.

If we never stand by the water
and get our feet wet,
then we will never know what it is
to place all things in your hands,
and be held completely by you.

May we step into the water and reach the other side:
into all conflict and cross towards peace;
into all hunger and cross towards the table;
into all injustice and cross towards full living.

Readings

Joshua 3:1–17	*Crossing the Jordan*
Exodus 14:22–9	*The parting of the Red Sea*
Psalm 22:1–11	*Trusting God*
Mark 6:45–52	*Calming of the storm*

Prayer Activity

Today as you journey, to work, to the shops, to visit someone, or even as you go from room to room in your own home, consider the crossing points – doorways, pavement edges, the change from bed to floor, bus to pavement, steps – and pause at each. Feel God's blessing as God crosses with you.

Prayer for the Church

Those who are concerned that the physical surroundings of the local church assist towards deeper worship, warmer hospitality and stronger witness

especially the Committee on Church Art and Architecture.

Blessing

May we have the courage
to step out into the unknown
knowing there is
no place, no danger, no challenge, no difficulty
that we cannot face
while we remain within your care.

VALLEY – FIELDS

At that time Jesus went through the grainfields on the sabbath; his disciples were hungry, and they began to pluck heads of grain and to eat. When the Pharisees saw it, they said to him, 'Look, your disciples are doing what is not lawful to do on the Sabbath.'

~ Matthew 12:1, 2 ~

Living Lord,
As I look out upon your world,
I see so many lives
That are stunted, constricted and blighted
By the rigidity of religion
And the pretensions of piety.

And then I look at Jesus
And see one who is gloriously
And marvellously free,
I see one who is Utterly human –
And yet God present to us,
The very Glory of God
Smiling out from a weathered face.

As the disciples cavort and caper
Their way through the cornfields,
(Breaking human regulations,
But fulfilling the law of God)
You show us your joy
Breaking in upon religion's sobriety,
Your festivity gate-crashing,
The dour gatherings of the smugly pious.

Lord, I pray that in my life
And in the life of the world,
There may be a true breakthrough
Of that humanity and liberty
Which mark the place
Where the Christ has walked.   AMEN.

Readings

Jeremiah 7:1–7   *Against empty religion*
James 1:26–7   *True religion*
Micah 6:6–8   *What God requires*
Matthew 21:28–32   *Parable of two sons*

Prayer Activity

Use your imagination. Piece together in your mind the scene of Jesus and his disciples in the cornfields. Imagine the landscape, the sights, the sounds, the smells. Now focus closer on Jesus and the disciples. Focus on how they are walking and on their facial expressions. Then do the same with Jesus' opponents. Reflect. Pray.

Prayer for the Church

Those who at all levels encourage and enable different branches of the Church to relate to and learn from each other and about the Gospel they share

especially the Committee on Ecumenical Relations and those involved in the Action for Churches Together in Scotland.

Blessing

God keep you warm in your caring
God keep you quiet in your listening
God keep you joyful in your serving.

VALLEY – DARKNESS

Even though I walk through the darkest valley, I will fear no evil: for you are with me.

~ Psalm 23:4 ~

In the dark I lie.

No light shines through the curtain, no dim image can be seen.
No height, no depth, no breadth
And yet so claustrophobic.
No one but me and I am scared.

Because the darkness is all around
Like solitary confinement,
I imagine what I cannot see.
What lurks, what might I touch if I move
And what might touch me?

The darkness feels like no way out – no way
And I am lost.

Now I understand the Psalmists song, God.
Words from the struggle, cries from the depths.
And I long to know that the darkness is not emptiness,
That it is filled with your presence
for you are with me.

Lord, hear my prayer that the darkness will not overcome;
And when the faintest of light is seen again
Let all my soul shout out in appreciation
for life and light that darkness can never put out.

In our struggle, in our loneliness, in our shame,
Christ be our light today.

Readings

Psalm 23   *Shepherding comfort*
Ezekiel 37:1–14   *Valley of dry bones*
1 John 1:5–10   *God is light*

Prayer Activity

Close the curtains of the room, having set up a candle or a small lamp ready to be lit. Take time in the darkness to reflect on what feelings and inner fears the lack of light touches. Focus on what is most problematic or most challenging and then, once the light is restored, consider how differently this issue appears. In the light, think about how we might bring light into the world as reflectors of the light of Christ.

Prayer for the Church

As it seeks new patterns of ministry and mission for the more effective use of personnel and a stronger interface with the community

especially those in new charge developments and changing patterns and situations ministry.

Blessing

Goodness and mercy,
Light and life,
Comfort and joy
Be yours through Christ our Lord.

Introduction to Town

Going into a town or city can be quite overwhelming – the roar of the traffic, the rush and push of people, the sheer volume of information from shop windows and adverts and signs. But the town is lively, for life goes on here. And so it was in bibilical towns too: market place and temple court; teaching and talking, working and meeting – people came together with God in the midst, and the Spirit of God transcends culture and nationality and activity, creating new movement and colour.

TOWN – REBUILDING

Then the Word of the Lord came by the prophet Haggai, saying: Is it a time for you yourselves to live in your panelled houses, while this house lies in ruins? Go up to the hills and bring wood and build the house, so that I may take pleasure in it and be honoured, says the Lord.

~ Haggai 1:3, 4, 8 ~

Lord,
There are times when you question our priorities,
When you challenge our complacency;
And undermine our desire for comfort.

As once you summoned your people
From their selfish preoccupations
To the urgent task of re-building the temple,
So also you call us to the hallowed work
Of rebuilding and renewal.

You summon us
To rebuild that which is in ruins,
To mend that which has been broken,
And to heal that which has been hurt.

As once you called the people to work together,
To labour on the ruins, family with family,
And neighbour with neighbour,
So you call us to the Kingdom's work.

Today I pray for the unity of the Church
In pursuing the common vision
Of a healed world:
The earth filled with your glory
As the waters cover the sea.

Readings

Haggai 1:1–11   *The call to rebuild the temple*
1 Peter 2:4–8   *A living temple*
Ezekiel 47:1–9   *Living water flowing from the temple*
Psalm 122   *A temple psalm*
John 2:13–22   *Cleansing of the temple*
Isaiah 2:1–4   *A vision of peace*

Prayer Activity

Take time to reflect on the theme of rebuilding. In your own congregation: what needs rebuilding? (Conversely, what needs to be demolished?) What is broken or hurting? Have you contributed to that hurt or brokenness? Reflect on how you can be part of the rebuilding/healing process.

You can do the same reflection in relation to your own family and community.

Prayer for the Church

Those who ensure that the fabric of church buildings is maintained and that the Church's heritage in buildings is conserved for the good of the Church and the nation

especially the General Trustees.

Blessing

The blessing of Christ the Master Builder be yours. May you be open to his gracious crafting as he makes a place for you in the living temple which is the Church.

TOWN – LONELINESS

Turn to me and be gracious to me, for I am lonely and afflicted.

~ Psalm 25:16 ~

So many people
So much loneliness
What a mystery.

When we cross the street to avoid someone, help us to listen our aversion;
Going deeper
Meditating on our reaction – is it prejudice?
What are we scared of – is it anything to do with them?
Is our avoidance a protection – and if so from what?
God, may thus our meeting again become healthier, more open, that I could be more
honest with myself and with you.

God, may I now face my deep loneliness, the leper within me,
The parts of myself I reject, that I do not want others to see, even you:
Is it so bad?
How can I befriend my own feelings of inadequacy,
The parts of myself I allow to get lonely and abandoned, so feeding my fears
Circling around in a downward spiral?

May I let you confront the parts of me that feel abandoned and check their reality
What I can change,
What I cannot change.
And may I have the wisdom to know the difference,
And the prayerfulness to dare to know myself,
Accept myself, open myself
Naked to your enfolding love,

Trusting you to bring the comfort that I need and the challenge.   AMEN.

Readings

2 Kings 5   *Naaman: could he obey?*

Luke 17:11–19   *One leper found complete wholeness of body, mind, emotion and spirit*

Luke 13:10–17   *Healing from isolation of her disability, affirmed as a woman*

Matthew 8:1–4   *Asking for what we need*

Prayer Activity

Most of the miracle stories of Jesus include some healing of emotions and bring social inclusion to people who were outcast. Think of any situation in which you feel lost, lonely, isolated, inadequate or misunderstood. Ask Christ to bring to your mind one of the miracle stories as 'medicine' for the situation you have thought about – and ponder – let Jesus' healing flow into you.

Prayer for the Church

The increasing number of people who choose to relate to the Church less through traditional membership patterns and more through general commitment and particular projects

especially Christian Aid and all agencies concerned with the homeless and healing of God's people.

Blessing

Open my heart to those I meet
Give me wisdom that I may greet
With the eyes of God
And the blessing of peace.

TOWN – POLITICS

Unless the Lord builds the house, those who build it labour in vain.
Unless the Lord watches over the city, the watchman stays awake in vain.

~ Psalm 127:1 ~

Blessed are you who came in the name of the Lord:
   fulfilling ancient prophecy,
   declaring in acted parable your kingship,
   coming not on some warhorse, but on a colt,
   proclaiming quietly, amid the tumult, peace,
   challenging the city of Jerusalem,
   upsetting the powers that be with another power.

Blessed are you who comes in the name of the Lord:
   God in Man and for Man.
   'Hosanna!' we echo the ancient cry.
   A word of real praise
   and a word of real prayer.
   'Hosanna!' Save us.
   Save us now and save us ever.
   Save us from acclaiming you on Sundays
     but forgetting you on Mondays.

Blessed are you who ever comes in the name of the Lord.
   Ride into our turbulent towns and cities:
     brighten their dark streets
     quelling every ugly passion.
   Enter the places of government
     disturb our leaders with your power
     reminding them of your peaceful programme.

Blessed are you who will come in the name of the Lord,
   Enable the Church, looking to the eternal city,
     to strive for your Kingdom on earth
     to be a citadel of hope on the edge of despair
     to work for the things that are of God as well as those of Caesar
     to pray for the peace of Jerusalem –

a vision in every parliament;
integrity among all politicians;
justice more than law in our courts;
honest enterprise in all public life;
and you our Redeemer King given the glory.   AMEN.

Readings

The triumphal entry into Jerusalem

> Matthew 21:1–11
> Mark 11:1–10
> Luke 19:28–40
> John 12:12–19

Prayer Activity

We often moan about the government – but when did we last pray specifically for politicians? Why not say a prayer today? When did we think about writing a letter or standing up for some political or social issue? Why not think to do something today when a subject concerns you?

Prayer for the Church

Those who steward the Church's financial resources and recall its members to the meaning of Christian giving

especially the Stewardship and Finance Committee and the General Treasurer's Department.

Blessing

> Lord, come away; why dost Thou stay?
> Thy road is ready and Thy paths made straight
> With long expectation wait the consecration of Thy beauteous feet.
> Ride on triumphantly: behold! we lay our lusts and proud wills in Thy way.

Jeremy Taylor (1613–67)

TOWN – CULTURES

…those who love God must love their brothers and sisters also.

~ I John 4:21 ~

On pavements packed with pushing people,
In cities that never sleep,
In the roar of traffic and the glare of lights,
You speak …
Love one another.

Among the streetwise and the tourists,
Between the natives and the immigrants,
Inside the shops and the restaurants,
You speak …
Love one another.

In the crowded square and the darkened alley,
In the gorgeous galleries and the dirty gutters,
In the noise of so many different languages,
You speak …
Love one another.

God of love,
In the honesty of labour and in the creativity of the Arts,
In the gathering of the nations and in integrated community
May *we* speak love, to one another.

Readings

Acts 2:1–13	*Pentecost unity*
Acts 16:11–34	*Diverse converts*
Galatians 3:23–9	*All children of God*
I Thessalonians 1:2–10	*Church thanksgiving*

Prayer Activity

If you have a hymn book at home, flick through it until you find a hymn from another country and culture. Alternatively, open your kitchen cupboard and find foods or ingredients from other places and traditions. Think about the new flavours and styles these other cultures have given you and thank God for the variety and diversity that enriches our world.

Prayer for the Church

Those who encourage and assist congregations to explore and develop patterns of life and mission appropriate to their own context

especially the Parish Development Fund Committee and the Scottish Churches Community Trust

Blessing

Welcome the stranger,
Learn from another,
Give thanks for the different ...
Speak the love God speaks for you.

Introduction to Beach

They are always thin places, beaches. There are no straight lines, only curves; even the horizon curves gently leading to new adventures and unknowns. It is also a border area from sea to land, from danger to safety. So much biblical thought understands the sea as a dangerous place filled with Leviathan and other monsters. Yet in this crossing point Jesus first meets the first disciples to call them and then after the adventure to share breakfast with them, resurrected. Here he also teaches crowds and feeds the 5,000. So, not just in a physical way are beaches border points but also spiritually where transformation takes place and the Realm of God begins to break open in us. Clearly it is not the only place this can happen, but it seems to be one place where it readily happens. Who knows why that is? Maybe it is the idea of walking on all those sand grain promises first given to Abraham; maybe it is the water's primal call from creation as the waves surround us; or maybe it is the fear of the sea on one side and the fear of the jungle on the other that finds us in a thin place where we are invited to pause and reflect and recognise a new truth, a deeper question or a blessing of God wandering there too, leaving footprints in the sand …

BEACH – CALLING

And Jesus said to them, 'Follow me and I will make you fish for people.'

~ Mark 1:17 ~

Where the waves lapped against the shore,
as salty, sandy hands tugged at nets and slippery fish,
when the working day was in full swing,
Jesus came, and the familiar was soon cast aside.

And yet, God, it seems so absurd that those men downed tools and followed your son.

What convinced them?
What made them leave so much and take up so much?
Today we, too, grapple with that challenge.

So help us recognise that compelling communication you had and have with your
    people,
for in Jesus you spoke to the heart of working communities;
farmers and fishers, those who worked with their hands;
you spoke and they understood beyond words,
hearing you the maker and the worker of wonders.

So that's the call to us today too, typists and teachers, scientists and social workers ...

Maybe not to down tools ...
but to bring your transforming presence into what we are already doing.

To notice that, as we teach – we hear the patience of Jesus,
As we write – we know the creativity of Spirit,
As we care – we nurture your compassion,
As we make and communicate and order – we begin again our journey
where something in you overwhelms something in us,
making us follow no matter what or where.

Readings

Jonah 3:1–5, 10 *A reluctant response*
Mark 1:14–20 *Answering the call*
Luke 8:4–8 *Listen if you have ears*

Prayer Activity

Reflect on three very different ways people earn a living, for example, by working with their hands as a joiner or builder, using their minds as researcher or technician or by expressing creativity as designer or artist. How might God speak to them in these tasks? What do you do that links you to the nature of God without words and what qualities from God do you need to work today?

Prayer for the Church

Those who offer special expertise to local congregations as they seek to develop their work, worship and witness

especially the Regional Development Officers of the Mission and Discipleship Council.

Blessing

Unspoken love;
Let us begin with new things,
Let us break from old things;
Let us behold your things, in all ways this day.

BEACH – FOLLOWING –VISIONS – RESURRECTION SIGHTINGS

Just as day was breaking, Jesus stood on the beach; yet the disciples did not know that it was Jesus.

~ John 21:4 ~

Lord, we believe: help our unbelief.
  The disciples did not recognise you at first.
No wonder – you were the last thing they expected;
  but you made yourself known
    as at the beginning, by the seashore.
Lord, come to us in your risen power in the everyday:
  as day breaks to give us new life and new hope,
  in our work to give us patience and perseverance.

Lord, we believe: help our unbelief:
  seeing not as Moses did at the burning bush
  hearing not as the disciples did beside the sea
yet in the here and now
    to turn aside with the eye of faith to behold the great sight
    to take the plunge and acclaim you
'It is the Lord' –
    God in the midst.
    God with us – great and glorious wonder.

Lord, we believe: help our unbelief.
  With all our great islands of knowledge
    there are yet longer shorelines
    which blind unbelief cannot scan.
Help all people to discern you – in the midst, yes;
  and on the edges and the horizons of living,
    Lord of science and of all things.

Lord, we believe: help our unbelief.
  As we would venture in faith in you,
    when the sands of time run out

leave us not on the beach,
but take us to the eternal shore
to see you face to face and acclaim you
the risen and glorious saviour.   AMEN.

Readings

Exodus 3:1–6   *Moses and the burning bush*
John 21:1–8   *The risen Jesus appears by the Sea of Galilee*

Prayer Activity

Think of a shore – of sand ... of shingle ... of stones: warm and pleasant or cold and wet. Comfortable or uncomfortable – an illustration of life. Howsoever, know that the Risen Jesus stands on whatever beach – with you always.

Prayer for the Church

As it meets in local Church councils where support is given and policies made

especially the Presbyteries, their Moderators and Clerks; Kirk Sessions and Session Clerks; Congregational Boards, Committees of Management, Deacons' Courts and their Clerks.

Blessing

Profound promise of the rising sun
deep peace of the risen Son
be mine this day and always.   AMEN.

BEACH – DAWNING

Jesus said to them, 'Come and eat.'
~ John 21:12 ~

The new dawn shakes its self awake,
pulling apart the night with yellows and golds;
and in the freshness of this thin light,
the beach seems crowded with resurrection.

Here on the edge of things:
between shore and land;
between dark and light;
between home and adventure;
I meet you face to face,
and staring into eyes
that confront me with images of crucifixion and death,
of darkness and things unimaginable,

I can see beyond,
as you have done,
into a reflection clear with the new promise of eternity,
and with sand between my toes,
the smell of fish on my fingers,
spray on my face,
and salt in my mouth,
we share a makeshift breakfast –
a sacramental moment,
that builds with light,
and truth,
and love,
for in my heart I know,
you are alive!

May every morsel I share with the world this day,
contain as much Good News as this.

Readings

John 21:1–14 *Breakfast on the beach*
Mark 1:14–20 *Calling of the fisherfolk*
John 21:15–19 *Feed my lambs*

Prayer Activity

Be there on that beach. Feel the smells and the sounds, the sun or wind on your face. Take yourself towards a small beach-fire and there is Jesus preparing breakfast. Eat with him. What would you say to him? What does he say to you?

Prayer for the Church

Those involved in Christian counselling and healing

especially the Christian Fellowship of Healing and other similar groups, and any local group in your church or area.

Blessing

May you find heaven crammed into every morsel.
May you find light in every dawn.
May you find good news in every conversation.
And may you find the Resurrected Lord smiling from every face.

BEACH – NOURISHING

Then Jesus ordered the crowds to sit down on the grass. Taking the five loaves and the two fish, he looked up to heaven, and blessed and broke the loaves, and gave them to the disciples, and the disciples gave them to the crowds.

~ Matthew 14:19 ~

Lord,
In my mind's eye,
I see them spread across the beach,
A great sea of humanity:

The smug and the struggling
The respectable and the reprobate
The pious and the perplexed

I see them in their diversity.

Yet I also see them even if only for
A timeless moment,
Under the blessing hands of Christ
Woven into one garment,
Fashioned into one people.

Did the smug and the struggling touch hands
As bread was broken?
Did the respectable and the reprobate
Look into each other's eyes
As fish was passed around?
Did the pious and the perplexed
Recognise in each other a shared longing?

Lord, today I pray for my own congregation.
May we who are so like that crowd on the hillside
Be fashioned by the hands of Christ
Into a sign of hope for a despairing world.   AMEN.

Readings

Matthew 25:31–40	*I was hungry*
Exodus 16:13–21	*Bread from heaven*
John 6:35–40	*Jesus, the Bread of Life*
Deuteronomy 8:1–3	*Not by bread alone*
Mark 14:17–25	*The Lord's Supper*
Luke 24:28–35	*Christ recognised in the breaking of the bread*

Prayer Activity

Place a loaf of bread on your prayer corner. Touch it, smell it. Think of the labour that went into producing it – from the farmer to the baker. Think of the nourishment it brings. Think of those who have no bread. Meditate on Jesus' words, 'I am the Bread of Life'.

Prayer for the Church

As it seeks to develop its spiritual life and become more aware of the God who is in all things and who is with us in our daily lives

especially those developing prayer networks and new initiatives in the support of community spiritual life.

Blessing

Christ who is the Bread of Life
Sustain you in the desert,
Strengthen you on the road,
And satisfy you at his table.

Introduction to Garden

There is an image often portrayed in medieval paintings of Jesus in the garden of resurrection. In that early morning light, just as Mary sees him for the first time, he is carrying a hoe over his shoulder. And indeed Mary imagines he is the gardener. But this is in fact true. As the creation story tells us, the First Ones were expelled from the garden but now that love has brought resurrection, the gardener has been restored to the garden. Love has brought balance again, restoring things the way God longed them always to be through Jesus' resurrection.

So gardens are places of discovery. And we are invited to walk there, and in so many ways, journey through the complete story of God. For in such places we discover image after image of the promise of new life, we can reflect on the trees that hold so much life, of birds in the oak's branches revealing a picture of the realm of heaven, of lilies and how they are clothed in such simple beauty, and of the darker places where Jesus prayed on that fateful Thursday evening following Passover. The whole story of faith can be lived in the garden. And God, the creator of all, has filled it with blessing.

GARDEN – CREATING

*And the L*ORD *God planted a garden in Eden, in the east; and there he put the man whom he had formed. Out of the ground the L*ORD *God made to grow every tree that is pleasant to the sight and good for food, the tree of life also in the midst of the garden, and the tree of the knowledge of good and evil.*

~ Genesis 2:8, 9 ~

Living God,
Today I remember

That you
Are in the business of planting,
Of sowing that seed
Which births fruitfulness and life.

Today I remember

That Eden is not so much
A lost garden from the ancient past,
As one that beckons to us
From the emergent future.

Today I remember

That you have set us here
To work with you
Towards that future,
As stewards of the earth
And not as owners.

Today I pray
For all who seek to cherish
The earth that you have
Put into our hands.

Readings

Genesis 2:4–17   *The Garden of Eden*
Luke 23:32–43   *The Penitent Thief and the promise of paradise*
Revelation 22:1–5   *The blessings of paradise*
Jeremiah 31:10–14   *God's people as a watered garden*
Mark 14:32–8   *The garden of Gethsemane*

Prayer Activity

Set in your prayer corner a growing plant. Read Psalm 1. Meditate on the theme of roots and fruits in your own life.

Prayer for the Church

Centres to which people may withdraw to renew body and mind and to engage more deeply in worship and study, seeking the relevance of the Gospel for the modern world

especially all retreat centres and places of calm and quiet in a busy world, providing rest and recreation of the spirit.

Blessing

May the Word of Christ
sink deep into your heart,
bringing forth life and fruitfulness
in due season.

GARDEN – LOVING

I have entered my garden, my sweetheart, my bride.
I am gathering my spices and myrrh;
I am eating my honey and honeycomb.

~ Song of Songs 5:1 ~

Tell me,
who would take an eternity
choosing the million flavours of peach
and not notice it pass?
Only you, my Creator.
Who would consider the patience it takes
to harmonise the subtleties of a flower's perfume
time well spent?
Only you, my Creator.
Who would celebrate that it took not a moment sooner
to compose the sound of bird song?
Only you, my Creator.

Creator,
may I find time to celebrate in your garden of wonder,
to slow down this moment of heaven
that sweeps me off my feet in love for you
from some holy recognition
too deep for words.

And if a burden is too great,
or a pain too fresh,
may that same garden wait for me
to bloom once more
into the life you shape for me,
that I might see in the waiting
the place of resurrection
calling me.

Readings

Song of Solomon 4:16–5:1	*The beloved comes to his garden*
Song of Solomon 5:10–16	*A portrait of the beloved*
Psalm 8	*God's glory and human worth*
Psalm 104	*In praise of the creator*
Job 38:2–15	*Were you there …*

Prayer Activity

Imagine the life of a single flower and its life cycle, watching it grow day by day and then die and give up its life. Reflect on the cross and what Jesus did for us all, giving his own life. The dead flower now waits for its seed to grow a new shoot, a new plant to burst through the ground: imagine Jesus in the tomb about to do the same.

Prayer for the Church

Those who are in my own congregation, helping it to be part of the living, witnessing Church

especially those who challenge me and my brothers and sisters into fresh new adventures of witness and mission.

Blessing

May you see love around you.
May you feel love walk with you.
May you know love holds you.
And may you hear love speak your name.

GARDEN – RECOGNISING

Supposing him to be the gardener, she said to him, 'Sir, if you have carried him away, tell me where ...'

~ John 20:15 ~

Lord God,
It was on a green hill far away that we think of you on that cross.
A red bloody day when the sky turned black ...
but on a green hill.
And when you stood before Mary on that first Easter day
We think of you in the green garden with the empty tomb –
Not because the scenery is described but because you are:
And you were thought to be the gardener.

In the garden of your world, God,
We build things out of things you grew.
We snatch at life that has taken time to be.
We trample on detail and intimate design
And hammer a cross to stand on a green hill.

But beneath it all and about it all is your greenery, God,
Your life force to be reckoned with,
Your breath blowing butterflies in the breeze,
Your water of life nourishing and replenishing,
Your sun warming and comforting seed and creature.

Yes, you are the gardener, God,
Down to earth – planting and pruning
But waiting patiently too
For Mary, and us
to recognise the gardener,
Then hear the teacher,
then receive the saviour.

Readings

John 20:11–18   *In the garden*
Genesis 2:10–17   *The Garden of Eden*

Prayer Activity

Take some old photographs of people you know, especially family, and look at them. Trying to see particular characteristics or immediately recognisable features. What things have changed over the years and what makes them instantly recognisable? How do we overcome our lack of recognition of Jesus in those around us?

Prayer for the Church

My own part in the Church and the special gifts I have been given which, in unity with others, build up the body of Christ

especially the forgotten skills and abilities, those which may lead me into new and exciting adventures of faith.

Blessing

The tending of the gardener,
The wisdom of the teacher,
The hope of the saviour
Is with us all, through Christ our Lord.   AMEN.

Daily Bible Readings

The asterisk* denotes the following Sunday's readings and psalm proscribed in the Revised Common Lectionary (and as in *Common Order*), and the readings set for special festivals.

These readings come from the Australian publication, *With Love to the* World, a daily Bible reading guide prepared in the Uniting Church in Australia and used throughout Australia and increasingly world-wide. It contains short notes on each passage, by writers who are knowledgeable about the biblical background as well as other material. It is published quarterly. Copies can be ordered through the Church of Scotland's Office for Worship. Individual copies are £2.50 or an annual subscription is £10.00.

NOVEMBER 2006

Mon	20	John 18:33–37*
Tue	21	Revelation 1:4b–8*
Wed	22	Daniel 7:1, 9–14
Thu	23	Psalm 93
Fri	24	2 Samuel 22:1–16
Sat	25	2 Samuel 23:1–7*
Sun	26	Psalm 132:1–12,
		(13–18)*

Mon	27	1 Thessalonians 3: 9–13*
Tue	28	3 John 1–15
Wed	29	Luke 20:45—21:6, 20–24
Thu	30	Luke 21:25–38 (25–36*)

DECEMBER

Fri	1	Jeremiah 33:14–16*
Sat	2	Jeremiah 33:23–26

Sun	3	Psalm 25:1–10*
		First Sunday of Advent
Mon	4	Philippians 1:3–11*
Tue	5	2 Peter 3:1–9
Wed	6	Luke 3:1–6*
Thu	7	Zechariah 8:14–19
Fri	8	Malachi 3:1–4*
Sat	9	Psalm 126
Sun	10	Luke 1:68–79* Canticle

Mon	11	Philippians 4:4–7*
Tue	12	Revelation 3:7–13
Wed	13	Luke 3:7–18*
Thu	14	John 3:22–36
Fri	15	Zephaniah 1:14–18
Sat	16	Zephaniah 3:14–20*
Sun	17	Isaiah 12:1–6 (2–6*)
		Canticle

Mon	18	Hebrews 10:1–4	Mon	15	1 Corinthians 12:12–31a*
Tue	19	Hebrews 10:5–10*	Tue	16	1 Peter 1:10–16
Wed	20	Revelation 20:11–21:5	Wed	17	Isaiah 61:1–6
Thu	21	Luke 1:39–45 [39–45,	Thu	18	Luke 4:14–21*
		(46–55)*]	Fri	19	Ezra 7:1–16
Fri	22	Micah 5:2–5a*	Sat	20	Nehemiah 8:2–10 (1–3,
Sat	23	Psalm 80:1–7*			5–6, 8–10*)
Sun	24	Luke 2:1–20 (Christmas	Sun	21	Psalm 19*
		Eve)			
			Mon	22	1 Corinthians 13:1–13*
Mon	25	Christmas John 1:1–14	Tue	23	1 Corinthians 14:1–12
		Christmas Day	Wed	24	Jeremiah 1:4–10*
Tue	26	Hebrews 1:1–12	Thu	25	Jeremiah 1:11–19
		Christmas Day	Fri	26	Isaiah 32:1–8
Wed	27	1 John 3:1–12, 21–24			Australia Day
Thu	28	Colossians 3:12–17*	Sat	27	Luke 4:21–30*
Fri	29	Luke 2:41–52*	Sun	28	Psalm 71:1–6*
Sat	30	1 Samuel 2:18–20, 26*			
Sun	31	Psalm 148*	Mon	29	1 Corinthians 15:1–11*
			Tue	30	Genesis 13:14–18
			Wed	31	Luke 5:1–11*

JANUARY 2007

| Mon | 1 | Deuteronomy 11:1–17 |
| | | New Year |

FEBRUARY

Tue	2	Acts 8:14–17*	Thu	1	Galatians 3:15–22
Wed	3	Luke 3:15–17, 21–22*	Fri	2	Isaiah 6:1–8 [1–8,
Thu	4	Isaiah 43:1–7*			(9–13)*]
Fri	5	Psalm 72:1–7, 10–14*	Sat	3	Isaiah 6:9–13
		(for Epiphany)	Sun	4	Psalm 138*
		Epiphany of the Lord			
Sat	6	Ephesians 3:1–13	Mon	5	1 Corinthians 15:12–20*
		Epiphany	Tue	6	Isaiah 44:1–8
Sun	7	Psalm 29*	Wed	7	Luke 6:17–26*
			Thu	8	Luke 6:27–38
Mon	8	Ezekiel 36:22–28	Fri	9	Luke 6:39–49
Tue	9	1 Corinthians 12:1–11*	Sat	10	Jeremiah 17:5–10*
Wed	10	Galatians 2:1–10	Sun	11	Psalm 1*
Thu	11	John 2:1–11*			
Fri	12	Song of Songs 7:1–13	Mon	12	Genesis 45:3–11, 15
Sat	13	Isaiah 62:1–5*	Tue	13	1 Corinthians 15:35–50
Sun	14	Psalm 36:5–10*	Wed	14	2 Corinthians 3:12–4:2*

Thu	15	Luke 9:28–36 [28–36, (37–43)*]	Sat	17	Joshua 5:9–12*
Fri	16	John 12:27–41	Sun	18	Psalm 32*
Sat	17	Exodus 34:29–35*	Mon	19	Philippians 3:4b–14*
Sun	18	Psalm 99*	Tue	20	Romans 14:10–18
			Wed	21	John 8:1–11
Mon	19	Luke 4:1–13*	Thu	22	John 12:1–8*
Tue	20	Romans 9:30—10:8a	Fri	23	Luke 23:44–56
Wed	21	Ash Wed. Psalm 51:1–17	Sat	24	Isaiah 43:16–21*
		Ash Wednesday	Sun	25	Psalm 126*
Thu	22	Romans 10:8b–13*			
Fri	23	Luke 5:29–35	Mon	26	Luke 19:28–40 (*alt.) (Palm)
Sat	24	Deuteronomy 26:1–11*	Tue	27	Isaiah 50:4–9a* (Passion)
Sun	25	Psalm 91:1–6, 9–16 (1–2, 9–16*)	Wed	28	Psalm 31:9–16* (Passion)
			Thu	29	Philippians 2:5–11* (Passion)
Mon	26	Philippians 3:17—4:1*			
Tue	27	Jeremiah 26:1–6	Fri	30	Luke 22:47–62
Wed	28	Jeremiah 26:7–15	Sat	31	Luke 22:63—23:12

MARCH

Thu	1	Luke 13:31–35*
Fri	2	Acts 7:2–8, 51–53
Sat	3	Genesis 15:1–12, 17–18*
Sun	4	Psalm 27*
Mon	5	1 Corinthians 10:1–13*
Tue	6	1 Corinthians 10:14–31
Wed	7	Hebrews 3:12–19
Thu	8	Luke 13:1–9*
Fri	9	Exodus 3:1–15
Sat	10	Isaiah 55:1–9*
Sun	11	Psalm 63:1–8*
Mon	12	Hosea 3:1–5
Tue	13	2 Corinthians 5:6–15
Wed	14	2 Corinthians 5:16–21*
Thu	15	Luke 15:1–3, 11b–32*
Fri	16	Joshua 4:19–24

APRIL

Sun	1	Luke 23:13–43 (1–49*) (Passion) *Palm/Passion Sunday*
Mon	2	Isaiah 65:17–25 (* alt)
Tue	3	Psalm 118:1–2, 14–24*
Wed	4	1 Corinthians 15:19–26*
Thu	5	Luke 22:7–20 (Maundy Thursday)
Fri	6	John 18:17—19:42 (Good Friday) *Good Friday*
Sat	7	Luke 24:1–12*
Sun	8	Acts 10:34–43* *Easter Day*
Mon	9	Revelation 1:4–8*
Tue	10	Revelation 1:9–19
Wed	11	John 20:1–18 (Eas alt)

Thu	12	John 20:19–31*
Fri	13	Acts 5:12–16
Sat	14	Acts 5:27–32*
Sun	15	Psalm 150*
Mon	16	Revelation 5:1–10
Tue	17	Revelation 5:11–14*
Wed	18	John 21:1–14
Thu	19	John 21:15–19 (1–19*)
Fri	20	Acts 9:1–6* [1–6, (7–20)*]
Sat	21	Acts 9:7–20
Sun	22	Psalm 30*
Mon	23	Revelation 6:1–17
Tue	24	Revelation 7:9–17*
Wed	25	John 10:22–30*
Thu	26	Jeremiah 29:1, 4–13 (Anzac)
Fri	27	Acts 9:36–43*
Sat	28	Acts 13:15–16, 26–33
Sun	29	Psalm 23*
Mon	30	Revelation 21:1–6*

MAY

Tue	1	John 5:1–18 (Eas 6 alt)
Wed	2	John 13:31–35*
Thu	3	Acts 11:1–18*
Fri	4	Acts 13:44–52
Sat	5	Acts 14:8–18
Sun	6	Psalm 148*
Mon	7	Revelation 21:10–21 (21:10, 22—22:5*)
Tue	8	Revelation 21:22—22:5
Wed	9	Joel 2:21–27
Thu	10	John 14:23–29*
Fri	11	Acts 15:1–2, 22–29

Sat	12	Acts 16:9–15*
Sun	13	Psalm 67*
Mon	14	Revelation 22:12–21 (12–14, 16–17, 20–21*)
Tue	15	John 16:25–35
Wed	16	John 17:20–26*
Thu	17	Luke 24:44–53 (*Ascension) *Ascension of the Lord*
Fri	18	Acts 1:1–11
Sat	19	Acts 16:16–34*
Sun	20	Psalm 97*
Mon	21	Romans 8:14–17*
Tue	22	Genesis 11:1–9 (alt*)
Wed	23	Numbers 11:24–30
Thu	24	John 14:8–17*
Fri	25	Acts 2:1–13 (1–21*)
Sat	26	Acts 2:14–21
Sun	27	Psalm 104:24–34, 35b* *Pentecost*
Mon	28	Romans 5:1–5*
Tue	29	1 Peter 1:10–16
Wed	30	John 16:12–15*
Thu	31	Ezekiel 1:15—2:2

JUNE

Fri	1	Proverbs 8:1–4, 22–31*
Sat	2	Proverbs 8:32—9:10
Sun	3	Psalm 8*
Mon	4	1 Kings 17:8–16 [8–16, (17–24)]*
Tue	5	1 Kings 17:17–24
Wed	6	Galatians 1:1–10
Thu	7	Galatians 1:11–24*
Fri	8	Luke 7:1–10

Sat	9	Luke 7:11–17*
Sun	10	Psalm 146*
Mon	11	1 Kings 21:1–10, (11–14), 15–21a*
Tue	12	Galatians 2:1–14
Wed	13	Galatians 2:15–21*
Thu	14	Luke 7:18–23
Fri	15	Luke 7:24–35
Sat	16	Luke 7:36 — 8:3*
Sun	17	Psalm 5:1–8*
Mon	18	1 Kings 19:1–4, (5–7), 8–15a*
Tue	19	Galatians 3:6–18
Wed	20	Galatians 3:19–29 (23–29*)
Thu	21	Luke 8:4–15
Fri	22	Luke 8:16–21
Sat	23	Luke 8:26–39*
Sun	24	Psalms 42 and 43*
Mon	25	2 Kings 2:1–14 (1–2, 6–14*)
Tue	26	Galatians 4:1–7
Wed	27	Galatians 5:1, 13–26 (1, 13–25*)
Thu	28	Luke 8:40–56
Fri	29	Luke 9:1–6
Sat	30	Luke 9:51–62*

JULY

Sun	1	Psalm 77:1–2, 11–20*
Mon	2	2 Kings 5:1–14*
Tue	3	2 Kings 5:15–27
Wed	4	Galatians 6:1–10 [(1–6), 7–16*]
Thu	5	Galatians 6:11–18
Fri	6	Luke 10:1–11, 16–20*

Sat	7	Luke 10:21–24
Sun	8	Psalm 30*
Mon	9	Amos 7:7–17*
Tue	10	Colossians 1:1–8 (1–14*)
Wed	11	Colossians 1:9–14
Thu	12	Luke 10:25–37*
Fri	13	Psalm 25:1–10 (*alt)
Sat	14	Deuteronomy 30:9–14 (*alt)
Sun	15	Psalm 82*
Mon	16	Amos 8:1–12*
Tue	17	Colossians 1:15–23 (15–28*)
Wed	18	Colossians 1:24–29
Thu	19	Luke 10:38–42*
Fri	20	Psalm 15 (*alt)
Sat	21	Genesis 18:1–10a (*alt)
Sun	22	Psalm 52*
Mon	23	Hosea 1:2–10*
Tue	24	Colossians 2:6–15 [6–15, (16–19)*]
Wed	25	Colossians 2:16–19
Thu	26	Luke 11:1–13*
Fri	27	Luke 11:14–28
Sat	28	Luke 11:37–54
Sun	29	Psalm 85*
Mon	30	Hosea 11:1–11*
Tue	31	Luke 12:1–7

AUGUST

Wed	1	Luke 12:8–12
Thu	2	Luke 12:13–21*
Fri	3	Psalm 49:1–12 (*alt)

Sat	4	Colossians 3:1–11*	Mon	3	Jeremiah 18:1–11*
Sun	5	Psalm 107:1–9, 43*	Tue	4	Jeremiah 18:12–17
			Wed	5	Philemon 1–21*
Mon	6	Isaiah 1:1, 10–20*	Thu	6	Luke 14:25–33*
Tue	7	Hebrews 11:1–3, 8–16*	Fri	7	Deuteronomy 30:15–20 (*alt)
Wed	8	Luke 12:22–31	Sat	8	Psalm 1 (*alt)
Thu	9	Luke 12:32–40*	Sun	9	Psalm 139:1–6, 13–18*
Fri	10	Psalm 33:12–22 (*alt)			
Sat	11	Luke 12:41–48	Mon	10	Jeremiah 4:11–12, 22–28*
Sun	12	Psalm 50:1–8, 22–23*	Tue	11	1 Timothy 1:1–11
			Wed	12	1 Timothy 1:12–17*
Mon	13	Isaiah 5:1–7*	Thu	13	Luke 15:1–10*
Tue	14	Isaiah 5:8–17	Fri	14	Exodus 32:7–14 (*alt)
Wed	15	Hebrews 11:29—12:2*	Sat	15	Psalm 51:1–10 (*alt)
Thu	16	Luke 12:49–56*	Sun	16	Psalm 14*
Fri	17	Jeremiah 23:23–29 (*alt)			
Sat	18	Luke 13:1–9	Mon	17	Jeremiah 8:18—9:1*
Sun	19	Psalm 80:1–2, 8–19*	Tue	18	Jeremiah 9:12–16, 23–24
			Wed	19	1 Timothy 2:1–7*
Mon	20	Jeremiah 1:4–10*	Thu	20	1 Timothy 3:1–16
Tue	21	Jeremiah 1:11–19	Fri	21	Luke 16:1–13*
Wed	22	Hebrews 12:18–29*	Sat	22	Luke 16:14–18
Thu	23	Luke 13:10–17*	Sun	23	Psalm 79:1–9*
Fri	24	Psalm 103:1–8 (*alt)			
Sat	25	Luke 13:22–30	Mon	24	Jeremiah 32:1–3a, 6–15*
Sun	26	Psalm 71:1–6*	Tue	25	Jeremiah 36:1–4, 14b–24, 32
Mon	27	Jeremiah 2:1–13 (4–13*)	Wed	26	1 Timothy 4
Tue	28	Hebrews 13:1–8, 15–16*	Thu	27	1 Timothy 6:6–19*
Wed	29	Hebrews 13:17–25	Fri	28	Luke 16:19–31*
Thu	30	Luke 14:1, 7–14*	Sat	29	Amos 6:1a, 4–7
Fri	31	Psalm 112 (*alt)	Sun	30	Psalm 91:1–6, 14–16*

SEPTEMBER

Sat	1	Luke 14:15–24
Sun	2	Psalm 81:1, 10–16*

OCTOBER

Mon	1	Lamentations 1:1–6*
Tue	2	2 Timothy 1:1–14*

Wed	3	Luke 17:1–4
Thu	4	Luke 17:5–10*
Fri	5	Habakkuk 1:1–4; 2:1–4
		(*alt)
Sat	6	Lamentations 3:19–26*
Sun	7	Psalm 137*
Mon	8	Jeremiah 29:1, 4–7*
Tue	9	2 Timothy 2:8–15*
Wed	10	2 Timothy 2:16–26
Thu	11	Luke 17:11–19*
Fri	12	Psalm 111 (*alt)
Sat	13	Luke 17:20–37
Sun	14	Psalm 66:1–12*
Mon	15	2 Timothy 3:1–9
Tue	16	2 Timothy 3:10—4:5
		(3:14—4:5*)
Wed	17	Jeremiah 31:27–34*
Thu	18	Jeremiah 31:35–40
Fri	19	Luke 18:1–8*
Sat	20	Genesis 32:22–31
Sun	21	Psalm 119:97–104*
Mon	22	Joel 2:12–17
Tue	23	Joel 2:18–32 (23–32*)
Wed	24	2 Timothy 4:6–8, 16–22
		(6–8, 16–18*)
Thu	25	Luke 18:9–14*
Fri	26	Luke 18:15–17
Sat	27	Luke 18:18–30
Sun	28	Psalm 65*
Mon	29	Habakkuk 1:1–4; 2:1–4*
Tue	30	2 Thessalonians 1:1–12
		(1–4, 11–12*)

| Wed | 31 | Ephesians 1:11–23 |
| | | (*alt All Saints) |

NOVEMBER

Thu	1	Luke 6:20–31
		(*All Saints Day)
Fri	2	Luke 18:35–43
Sat	3	Luke 19:1–10*
Sun	4	Psalm 119:137–144*
Mon	5	Haggai 1:15b—2:9*
Tue	6	2 Thessalonians 2:1–5,
		13–17*
Wed	7	Luke 20:27–38*
Thu	8	Job 19:23–27a*
Fri	9	Zechariah 10:6–12
Sat	10	Psalm 98*
Sun	11	Psalm 145:1–5, 17–21*
Mon	12	Isaiah 65:17–25*
Tue	13	2 Thessalonians 3:1–5
Wed	14	2 Thessalonians 3:6–13*
Thu	15	Zephaniah 3:14–20
Fri	16	Luke 21:5–19*
Sat	17	Luke 21:29–36
Sun	18	Isaiah 12*
Mon	19	Jeremiah 23:1–6*
Tue	20	Colossians 1:11–20*
Wed	21	Luke 23:33–43*
Thu	22	1 Corinthians 15:19–28
Fri	23	Deuteronomy 17:14–20
Sat	24	Psalm 46 (*alt)
Sun	25	Luke 1:68–79*
		Christ the King

Serving Overseas with the Church of Scotland
with their families
(to be added to the Prayer for the Church for each day)

Day 1   MALAWI: Andy and Felicity Gaston with Katy and Daniel
Day 2   MALAWI: Helen Scott
Day 3   ZAMBIA: Colin Johnston
Day 4   KENYA: Alison Wilkinson
Day 5   FRANCE: Alan and Lucie Miller
Day 6   CENTRAL ASIA: Alastair and Mary Morrice
Day 7   ISRAEL: Antony and Darya Short, with Joelle and Ezra
Day 8   TRINIDAD: John Garwell and Claudette Bacchas with Kerri-Ann
Day 9   ISRAEL: Jane and Ian Barron
Day 10   ISRAEL AND PALESTINE: Jeneffer Zielinski
Day 11   ISRAEL AND PALESTINE: John and Moira Cubie
Day 12   BANGLADESH: David and Sarah Hall
Day 13   BANGLADESH: Helen Brannam
Day 14   ISRAEL AND PALESTINE: Gwen and Mark Thompson
Day 15   JAMAICA: Margaret Fowler
Day 16   SRI LANKA: John and Patricia Purves
Day 17   BERMUDA: Alan and Elizabeth Garrity
Day 18   BAHAMAS: Scott and Anita Kirkland with Priscilla and Sarah
Day 19   COSTA DEL SOL: John and Jeannie Shedden
Day 20   ROTTERDAM: Robert and Lesley-Ann Calvert with Simeon, Zoe, Benjamin and Daniel
Day 21   ROME: William and Jean McCulloch with Jennifer
Day 22   AMSTERDAM: John and Gillian Cowie with Matthew, Sarah and Ruth
Day 23   BANGLADESH: James Pender
Day 24   LAUSANNE: Melvyn and Doreen Wood with Calum
Day 25   GIBRALTAR: Stewart and Lara Lamont
Day 26   GENEVA: Ian and Roberta Manson with Andrew, Robert and David
Day 27   BELGIUM: Matthew Ross
Day 28   BRUSSELS: Andrew and Julie Gardner
Day 29   MALTA: David and Jackie Morris
Day 30   BAHAMAS: Terry and Virginia Purvis-Smith
Day 31   PORTUGAL: William and Maureen Ross

Acknowledgements

Scriptural quotations, unless otherwise stated, are from the *New Revised Standard Version,* © 1989 Division of Christian Education of the National Council of the Churches of Christ in the United States of America, published by Oxford University Press.

The blessings at the conclusion of each day, whose sources are given, are reproduced by permission.

Blessing, page 23 – Amy Carmichael (1867–1951), *Towards Jerusalem* (SPCK, 1967)
Blessing, page 37 – David Adams, *Borderlands*, p. 3 (SPCK, 1991)

The list of Daily Bible Readings is from *With Love to the World* and is reproduced by kind permission.

Pray Now 2007 was prepared by members of the Pray Now Group: Gayle Taylor, Roddy Hamilton, Douglas Lamb, Jenny Williams and Jim Campbell.

For further information about *Pray Now* and other publications from the Office for Worship and Doctrine, contact:

> Office for Worship and Doctrine
> Mission and Discipleship Council
> Church of Scotland
> 121 George Street
> Edinburgh EH2 4YN
> Tel: 0131 225 5722 ext. 359
> Fax: 0131 220 3113
> e-mail: wordoc@cofscotland.org.uk

We gratefully acknowledge the following for their kind permission to reproduce the pictures used in this book: Bill Kean, Tom MacDonald, Gayle Taylor, Jenny Williams and Roddy Hamilton.